Careers in Forensics ™

Careers in
Ballistics Investigation

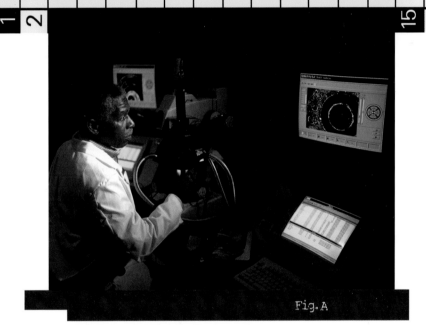

Fig. A

Janell Broyles
with
Matthew Broyles

rosen publishing's
rosen
central

New York

To Dean, for all the help

Published in 2008 by The Rosen Publishing Group, Inc.
29 East 21st Street, New York, NY 10010

Library of Congress Cataloging-in-Publication Data

Broyles, Janell.
Ballistics / Janell Broyles with Matthew Broyles.—1st ed.
     p.cm.—(Careers in forensics)
Includes bibliographical references and index.
ISBN-13: 978-1-4042-1345-6 (library binding)
1. Forensic ballistics—United States. I. Broyles, Matthew. II. Title.
HV8077.B76 2008
363.25'62—dc22

                                                                    2007033465

Manufactured in the United States of America

On the cover: A ballistics expert examines the markings on a bullet under a microscope.

Contents

The first call came in at 7:15 AM. Gunfire was reported at the West Ambler Johnston Hall dormitory at Virginia Tech University. An unknown shooter had killed two people. Police rushed to the scene, believing the shooting to be an isolated incident. The university administration, thinking the danger had passed, sent an e-mail to the campus community telling everyone to keep an eye out for anything suspicious.

Then, at 9:45, a new set of calls came; another shooter, or the same one, was terrorizing students and teachers at Norris Hall, on the other side of campus. By the time police got there, the gunman had killed thirty-one people and taken his own life.

In the fear and confusion surrounding the first reports of the shootings at Virginia Tech on April 16, 2007, little was known for sure: how many dead and wounded there were, who the gunman was, and what his motive could possibly be for taking lives. At first, police were not even sure that there was only one killer, or that the two incidents were related, since the shootings occurred on different ends of the campus.

Police officers run out of Norris Hall on the Virginia Tech campus on April 16, 2007. Police had been caught off guard when the gunman opened fire at Norris Hall, since they believed the earlier shooting at the West Ambler dorm had been an isolated incident. Virginia governor Tom Kaine later created a panel to review police responses and procedures.

Within a day of the attacks, however, ballistics tests had proven that two weapons—a Glock 19 handgun and a semi-automatic Walther P22 pistol—had been fired at both locations. Fingerprinting revealed that the guns belonged to the dead shooter, Seung-Hui Cho. The findings were clear: there was no other gunman responsible for that tragedy.

Pictured here is a Glock 19 handgun, similar to that used by Seung-Hui Cho in the Virginia Tech shootings. The gun is being held by Roanoke Firearms store owner John Markell, who sold Cho his gun legally little more than a month before the shootings.

The Virginia Tech shootings provided a horrifying illustration of the central importance of ballistics to crime scene investigations and the methodologies used. Previous to this, most people's conception of the science of ballistics was drawn from television crime dramas. "Get me Ballistics!" barks the TV cop, and the next scene shows a man or woman in a lab coat bending over a microscope. "These two bullets don't match . . . it's not your guy!" says the scientist regretfully. That's the fictionalized version of what such an investigation looks like. But as you might suspect, there is a lot more to how ballistics is used in crime investigations than just a few minutes spent comparing bullet casings.

First of all, "ballistics" is a word you may hear tossed around a lot on TV shows and in the movies, but the kind of ballistics that is used to solve crime is called forensic ballistics. "Ballistics" by itself simply means the science that deals with the motion, behavior, and effects of projectiles. A projectile is anything that is thrown, hurled, fired, or launched. This can include bullets as well as rocks hurled by a catapult, baseballs thrown by a pitcher, and even rockets shot into space. Ballistics can also mean the science or art of designing and hurling projectiles in a way that will make them fly to a desired distance or height, or hit a specific target.

Forensic ballistics, on the other hand, is the science of analyzing firearm usage in crimes. It also involves analysis of bullets and bullet impacts at a crime scene to discover more information about a crime. Forensic ballistics investigation is a fascinating, demanding, and rewarding career choice. Dr. Zeno Geradts is a forensic scientist at the Netherlands Forensic Institute of the Ministry of Justice. He started out as a physicist but ended up working in ballistics and digital forensics. On his Web page, www.forensic.to, he lists reasons why you might want to become a forensics investigator. According to Geradts, the benefits include:

- The result of your work is visible and concrete.
- You have a high level of responsibility.
- Every case is unique.
- It can be interesting to work in a forensic laboratory with investigators from different fields, implement and validate new techniques, and do joint research with colleagues.

Yet Geradts is clear-eyed about the downside of his profession. He says that distasteful, difficult, and tedious aspects of the job include:

- Some criminal cases can have a strong impact on you emotionally.
- Your workload can get very heavy at times.
- You can spend a lot of time waiting to be called into court-rooms at inconvenient times.
- Because keeping good records is so important, you will have to do a lot of paperwork.
- Sometimes you may have to deal with calls or e-mails from reporters while you're working on an investigation or during the trial phase of a criminal case.
- You have to deal with criticism and cross-examination of your work.
- You might have to admit that you drew a wrong conclusion.
- You might not always get to use an investigative technique you want if it is not considered valid in the courtroom.

Like any career, forensic ballistics investigation has its challenges. However, the rewards and excitement of helping to solve crimes make it an attractive career for many scientists and law enforcement professionals.

Solving Crimes with Forensic Ballistics

Mathematicians and scientists have always been interested in the questions of ballistics, such as calculating the trajectories and speed of moving objects. Forensic ballistics, however, could not exist as a science until the invention and widespread use of gunpowder and firearms.

Gunpowder was invented in China in the ninth century CE. It was often used in harmless ways, such as for fireworks. But because it could explode so powerfully, many sought to find ways to use it as a weapon. The weapons invented included flamethrowers, cannons, and various projectiles that all used gunpowder as a fuel and caused explosions or destructive fires in battle. As early as the 1100s, long before guns were invented in the West, the Chinese had developed a basic firearm.

It was in Europe in the late 1400s, however, that a type of "handheld cannon" was first invented; it was the forerunner of the modern gun. Guns became popular as weapons of war. Soldiers returning from war brought their guns with them, and the weapons began to circulate among the general population, who generally used them

At left, a muzzle-loading rifle is loaded with gunpowder. Before the invention of bullet cartridges, early guns were loaded through the muzzle. This was a time-consuming and slow process and made guns less effective as weapons of war.

for hunting and defense of property. It was at this time in history that there first began to be records of guns being used in crimes.

Early Crime Solving Through Forensics

In 1794, in Lancashire, England, a surgeon was called to examine the body of a gunshot victim. He discovered a wad of paper in one of the wounds. (Guns at that time were loaded by stuffing bullets into the barrel with wads of paper and gunpowder.) The surgeon opened up the paper and found it was a torn piece of sheet music. When a suspect was arrested, sheet music with a piece torn out was found in his coat. The piece of paper taken

Calvin Goddard, the Father of Forensic Ballistics

1
2
3
4
5
6
7
8
9
10
11
12
13
14
15
16
17
18
19
20

The term "forensic ballistics" was coined by Colonel Calvin Hooker Goddard (1891–1955). During his distinguished career, Goddard was an army officer, an academic, a researcher, and a pioneer in forensic ballistics.

In April 1925, Goddard helped establish the Bureau of Forensic Ballistics in New York City, the first independent criminological laboratory in the United States. It was formed to provide firearms identification services through-out America. Goddard researched, wrote, and lectured extensively on the subject of forensic ballistics and firearms identification. The bureau was one of the first places to bring ballistics, fingerprinting, blood analysis, and trace evidence under one roof, revolutionizing the criminal sciences.

Goddard's professionalism, reliability, and use of a scientific method set a standard for the emerging field of forensic firearm identification. His testimony in several important trials paved the way for judicial acceptance of firearms identification. With his support, one of the bureau's cofounders, Philip O. Gravelle, developed the comparison microscope for the identification of fired bullets and cartridge cases. It was a major progression in the forensic science of firearms identification.

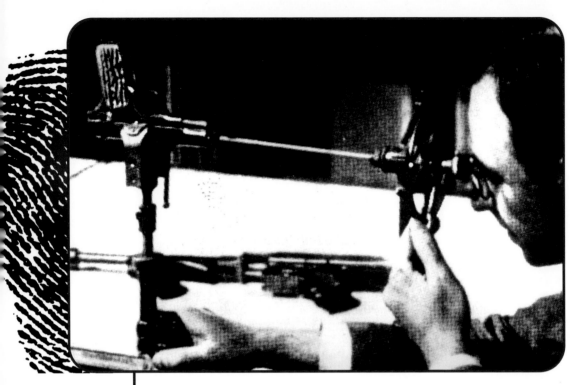

Calvin Goddard inspects a gun barrel in connection with the case of Nicola Sacco and Bartolomeo Vanzetti. Their trial for murder was one of the great legal controversies of the 1920s, despite some strong forensic evidence against them.

from the victim's wound matched the suspect's torn sheet music. The suspect was convicted, and the science of forensic investigation took an important step forward.

Nowadays, both the weapons used in crimes and the methods employed to identify them are more sophisticated, but the basic detective work largely remains the same. Like the eighteenth-century surgeon, today's ballistics investigators and other forensic professionals need to have a keen eye for detail.

Forensic Ballistics Helps Stop the Son of Sam

In January 1977, police in New York City began to suspect that one person was behind a string of handgun attacks that had left three people dead and several wounded. Investigation of the victims' wounds, as well as bullet holes and spent casings from the crime scenes, revealed that the killer had used a .44 Charter Arms Bulldog revolver, a type of gun that was fairly unusual. This was the police detectives' first bit of hard evidence. Meanwhile, the police and certain newspaper columnists began to receive letters allegedly written by the killer, who called himself the "Son of Sam." In these letters, the man that local tabloids began referring to as the ".44-Caliber Killer" promised there would be more killings unless he were to be stopped soon by the New York Police Department (NYPD), which he taunted and insulted.

When later clues and tips led police to a man named David Berkowitz, officers searched his car and found a .44-caliber revolver that matched the kind used to kill the Son of Sam victims. Ballistics tests showed that this gun had fired the shots that killed Stacy Moskowitz, one of the many victims targeted by the shooter. Berkowitz quickly confessed. He is currently serving time for his crimes. Even though there is still debate and speculation about whether he acted alone, the forensic evidence compiled by the NYPD means that Berkowitz's involvement in the crimes—and possession of the gun that was used to commit them—are no longer in question.

Ballistics Provides Just One of Many Clues

Many criminal cases have relied on ballistics evidence to catch and convict killers. However, since ballistics can tell us only what kind of weapon and ammunition were used and not necessarily who used them, ballistics data almost always have to be supplemented with other pieces of convincing or conclusive evidence.

In 1967, Donna Branion was found murdered in her home in Chicago, Illinois. Her husband, Dr. John Branion, called the police, saying he had come home from picking up their son at school to find her dead. During the examination of the crime scene and her autopsy, it was found that she had been shot by a .38 Walther PPK, an atypical handgun with distinctive rifling marks on the bullets. Dr. Branion had a gun collection but none of his guns matched this weapon.

As there had been no forced entry, robbery, or apparent enemies who would have targeted Mrs. Branion, police were baffled. However, indications of trouble in the couple's marriage turned suspicion on the husband. A search of their apartment turned

A New York City police detective displays the .44 Charter Arms Bulldog that "Son of Sam" serial killer David Berkowitz allegedly used in his string of murders in the 1970s. Since it was an unusual gun type at the time, ballistics evidence was especially helpful in identifying it as the murder weapon.

up a brochure for a Walther PPK, an extra clip of ammunition, and a practice target; all of these items bore a manufacturer's serial number. There was also a box of .38-caliber bullets matching the brand used in the murder, with four missing—the very same number of bullets fired at Donna Branion. Using the gun's unique identifying serial number, investigators were able to trace the gun to a store where a friend of Dr. Branion's had purchased it. This friend admitted giving it to Dr. Branion as a gift the year before.

Still not admitting guilt, the doctor now claimed that the assailants must have found and used his gun to kill his wife. The jury was not convinced, and he was convicted, even though the actual gun used to murder Donna Branion was never recovered.

Other famous cases have been derailed or shrouded in controversy due to incomplete or inconclusive ballistics evidence or by the discovery of clues that seem to tell a contradictory story. For example, the assassination of President John F. Kennedy in 1963 still inspires many conspiracy theorists who do not believe Lee Harvey Oswald was the only shooter. The bullets and fragments that were recovered do match the gun Oswald is believed to have used. But not all the bullets that hit the president were recovered, and the photographer who was allowed to take pictures of the exit wounds did not do a satisfactory job. The ballistic evidence is not conclusive enough to prove that there was only one shooter, so alternative theories about who really was involved in the killing of Kennedy continue to flourish.

Chapter

2 Forensic Ballistics Techniques

The American Academy of Forensic Scientists (AAFS) considers ballistics a part of the field of criminalistics. The academy says the main role of criminalists is to apply the physical and natural sciences to the examination and analysis of physical evidence. The kinds of evidence found at a crime scene—much of it very small, if not microscopic—can include hair, fibers (from clothes or carpets), bodily fluids, alcohol, drugs, paint smears or chips, broken glass, soil, leaf and grass debris, and traces of flammables. In addition to analyzing this trace evidence, criminalists will attempt to locate and record fingerprints and footprints, identify tool markings (perhaps as evidence of forced entry), and identify weapons used in a crime and compare bullets.

Once all this evidence is collected, safely transported to and stored in a secure laboratory, and examined and analyzed, the criminalist's findings and conclusions must be written up in a report that will be read by police officers, lawyers, and judges. In order to make it a useful and comprehensible document for these government officials,

A policeman picks up shell casings at the scene of a shooting. Shell casings, which often remain in good shape, can tell forensic ballistics experts quite a lot about the gun or guns used in a crime.

the criminalist must explain extremely technical details in everyday language that can be understood by everyone.

Though a fascinating and crucial job, criminal forensics is not easy. As AAFS points out on its Web site, "These types of analyses are difficult; they require an eye for detail, a broad practical scientific background, and the ability to apply these skills in the laboratory . . . Reconstructing the events of a crime is often very difficult. It requires an understanding of human behavior, of the physical laws and processes involved, and the recognition of how they interact."

Tasks of a Ballistics Expert

What a ballistics expert does day to day will vary depending on where he or she works. Small police departments may not have someone who can perform forensic ballistics examinations and instead will have to outsource these tasks to private labs, state agencies, or larger police departments. Federal investigation teams, on the other hand, might use many forensic ballistics experts to examine large crime scenes or work on high-profile cases.

Typical tasks that forensic ballistics investigators might perform include:

- Analyzing bullets and shell casings found at a crime scene
- Helping with crime scene reconstruction by working out the distance that bullets were fired from and their exact trajectory
- Matching a bullet or shell casing to a particular weapon or comparing it to a sample from another crime scene to see if the two are linked

Types of Bullets and Their Ballistic Properties

Knowing the various properties and types of bullets is essential for a forensic ballistics investigator. Bullets are usually made of lead or lead mixed with other metals. Because lead is a soft metal, bullets are often jacketed—or surrounded by a case of a harder metal—to keep them from losing their shape. A full metal jacket is a lead bullet totally enclosed in a harder metal. Some bullets are semi-jacketed, like hollow-point or soft-point bullets, so that

At left, a full metal jacket after it has been discharged; at right, an unfired bullet of the same type.

they will do more damage by splintering and spreading metallic fragments when they hit their target.

Handgun bullets are enclosed in cartridges, which are cases that contain the bullet, the propellant (some form of explosive powder, such as gunpowder), and the primer, a small amount of a chemical that will explode and light the explosive powder when the gun's firing pin hits it. Cartridges stay in the firing chamber or are ejected when the gun is fired.

Rifle bullets are similar to handgun bullets. But there are rifles called shotguns, and shotguns are not loaded with bullets. Shotguns are loaded with cartridges that contain shot—round pellets of metal—and these cartridges do more widespread damage to the target. Shot may come in various sizes, and shot size is one of the ways a bullet can be identified.

What a Bullet Reveals

Examining a bullet is not as simple as it sounds. Much of the time, there is no intact bullet to examine, only a damaged bullet or fragment of a bullet. However, it can still provide a great deal of information if the investigators do their job properly.

First, bullets have to be collected from a crime scene, without damaging them or altering them in any way. This can be hard to do when a bullet is lodged in a wall or inside a body. In addition, bullets can have trace evidence attached to them that must not be lost. Paint, fibers, fingerprints, and other materials—including flesh and blood—can cling to a fired bullet, giving investigators important clues.

Once bullets are collected, the forensic ballistics experts have to determine what type and caliber they are. While it is fairly easy to tell the difference between rifle bullets and handgun bullets, it may be harder to tell the difference between types of bullets fired from more similar guns.

Calibers and Gauges

Caliber is a measure of the approximate outside diameter, in inches, of a bullet cartridge, as well as of the inside diameter of a gun's barrel. In other words, a .22-caliber rifle has a barrel slightly less than a quarter of an inch—twenty-two hundredths of an inch—in diameter. The cartridges it shoots will also be approximately twenty-two hundredths of an inch in diameter. When caliber is measured in metrics, it is always stated in millimeters; a "9mm Luger" describes a well-known type of handgun that uses a metric caliber.

In addition to caliber, guns are categorized by other distinguishing characteristics, such as magnum (a term meaning higher-power gunpowder) or Colt (the gun's brand). There are many other gun name variations based on types of powder, bullet brand names, and other criteria, but being familiar with caliber types will give you a fairly good idea of a weapon's power.

Gauge is used to describe the types of shot used inside a shotgun cartridge. It indicates the number of spherical lead balls—each with a diameter equal to the inside diameter of the gun—that are required to total up to a pound of lead. The bigger the barrel of the rifle, the fewer balls it will take to reach a weight of a pound. Common gauges are 10-gauge, 12-gauge, 16-gauge, and 20-gauge shotguns.

Equipped with this basic knowledge of guns and bullets, a crime scene investigator may be able to determine what kind of shotgun was used by measuring and weighing all the shot pellets extracted from the scene and/or the victim. Twelve-gauge shot uses pellets that are about 0.05 inches in diameter, for example, while 00 shot, or "double-O" buckshot, has pellets about 0.33 inches in diameter.

Rifling

Most guns are rifled, meaning they have spiral grooves inside the barrel to make bullets spin as they are fired; this helps them to be

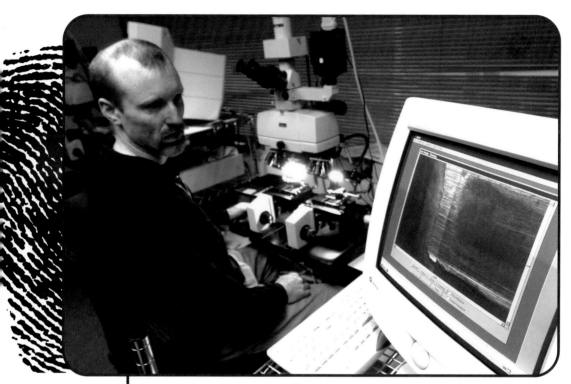

Travis Gover, Oregon State Police forensic scientist, uses a comparison microscope display on two bullets at a crime lab in 2003. Computer displays such as this one are a vast improvement on older techniques.

more accurate. The rifling grooves cut into the bullets as they spin. The grooves vary from manufacturer to manufacturer and gun to gun, making them useful for identifying the exact gun that shot a particular bullet. In fact, the Federal Bureau of Investigation (FBI) maintains a database called the General Rifling Characteristics File that helps forensic teams make those identifications.

Old firearms and shotguns that do not have this rifling are called smooth bore. They do not leave distinctive marks on bullets. They are also less accurate over longer firing distances due to the lack of bullet spin.

Shell Casings

Shell casings also have a story to tell, and an examiner can use many distinctive marks to identify them. These include:

- **Firing pin impression:** This tells investigators what kind of primer a shell used, narrowing down the potential gun types.
- **Breechblock patterns:** When powder in the bullet casing detonates and pushes the bullet down the barrel, the casing is forced against the breechblock, or the back of the firing chamber. This puts a dent in the casing that can be matched against a gun.
- **Headstamps:** This is a manufacturer's information that is stamped into a casing when it is made. Besides the brand name, headstamps can include the caliber, gauge, or shotgun type the bullet was made for.
- **Extractor and ejector marks:** In automatic and semiautomatic guns, extractors pull the next bullet from the clip and place it in the firing chamber, scratching it in the process. The same kinds of distinctive scratches are caused by ejectors that remove the used shell from the chamber and push it out of the weapon.

Trajectories and Wounds

Although "ballistics" refers to the trajectory of a hurled object, measuring bullet trajectories is really only one tool in the arsenal of a forensic ballistics investigator.

When a gun is fired, for example, it will expel gunpowder particles, and the presence or absence of these can tell a medical examiner how close the shooter stood to the victim. The farther away the two were, the fewer particles would settle on or near the victim's body. A more exact trajectory is often determined by firing the suspect weapon (a weapon believed to be the same as that used in the crime). The weapon is fired into materials similar to that the victim was wearing at a distance of six inches, one foot, eighteen inches, two feet, and three feet. The investigator then compares the residues the gun leaves behind with what was found on the victim. Whichever shooting distance creates a residue pattern that most closely approximates the pattern observed on the victim is probably the distance at which the victim was shot.

Analyzing gunshot wounds can reveal useful clues and infor-mation. The medical examiner performs this task but may need the help of a forensic ballistics investigator to confirm his or her conclusions. For example, if the medical examiner determines that a bullet passed through the victim's body instead of stopping inside it, but investigators were unable to find any bullets at the scene of the crime, this could indicate that the body may have been moved to a different location after the shooting.

Calculating the angle at which the bullets entered the body can tell investigators a lot about what was happening at the time of the crime, such as the shooter ambushing the victim from a tall hiding place or the victim struggling with the attacker before being shot. Analysis of the shooting angle may even help investigators find spent bullets that were initially overlooked at the scene.

Gunshot Residues

Gunshot residue (GSR) can provide revealing information even when there is no gun or bullet recovered at the crime scene. GSR can linger at the scene, on the victim, in vehicles that transported the victim, or on the clothes and skin of the person who fired the weapon. This allows investigators to make connections between the attacker and victim, and their movements and locations, as well as turn up new avenues to investigate.

GSR is caused when some of the primer and powder that cause the bullet to fire escape through openings in the gun. Revolvers in particular tend to leak GSR more than other types of guns. GSR is a tool of limited reliability, however, since it can blow onto innocent bystanders or anyone who picks up the gun later. It can also be washed away by rain.

Forensics experts find GSR by either observing it on clothes or skin, using infrared photography, or applying a method called a Griess test to analyze clothing or skin for residue.

Serial Numbers

Criminals typically file off a gun's serial numbers because they think this will keep the weapon from being identified by police. But serial numbers can be retrieved even if they are filed off. When a gun part is stamped with a serial number, even if the surface is filed, the metal that was stamped

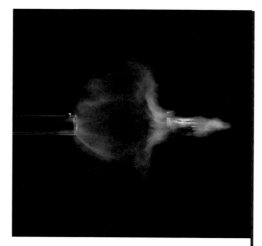

This discharge of a 12 bore shotgun bullet shows how, just four milliseconds after firing, a cloud of particles has begun to expand. This is what creates gunshot residue, which is a valuable clue in ballistics investigations.

still reveals structural changes. Forensics experts can detect the serial numbers through the use of several techniques:

- **Magnaflux:** Magnetizing the gun, which reveals ripples where the metal was stamped. Then the forensic examiner sprays oil that has iron particles in it on the ripples. The iron clings to the magnetized areas, making the serial number visible again. The advantage of this process is that it doesn't destroy the weapon.

- **Chemical and electrochemical etching:** A chemical solution is painted on the gun, which will etch the stamped area more than the unstamped area, making the numbers visible again. Using an electrical current to perform the chemical etching speeds the process. This method does do some damage to the gun and may destroy some evidence in the process.
- **Ultrasonic cavitation:** The gun is put in a special ultrasonic bath and exposed to high-frequency vibrations. This causes tiny bubbles to eat away at the gun, and they will eat away fastest at an area that has been stamped. Like etching, however, ultrasonic cavitation is also a potentially destructive process that can damage evidence.

Databases

With so much information to consider, it is not surprising that there are many databases a ballistics expert can use to make gun and bullet identifications. We have already mentioned the FBI's database on rifling, but there are others. They include:

- **IBIS (Integrated Ballistics Identification System):** The Bureau of Alcohol, Tobacco, Firearms, and Explosives maintains this database, which contains many bullets and shell casings found at crime scenes, enabling investigators to determine if a given weapon has been used at more than one crime.

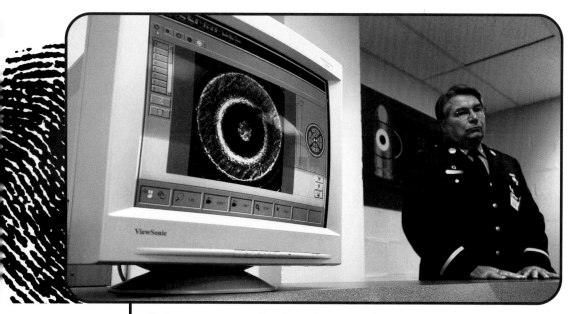

This computer display shows information stored by IBIS, the Integrated Ballistics Identification System. Maryland State Police colonel David Mitchell is demonstrating how it records a bullet's markings for ballistics comparisons.

- **DRUGFIRE:** DRUGFIRE is another database maintained by the FBI that focuses mainly on shell casings but also contains bullet records.

Bullet analysis, trajectory and wound analyses, gunshot residues, serial numbers, and gun and bullet databases are only a few of the techniques a forensic ballistics expert might employ when trying to determine if a weapon was used in a crime, what gun a bullet came from, what were the circumstances and actions surrounding the shooting, and who may have pulled the trigger. With every new technology that becomes available to criminal investigators, ballistics experts have new skills to learn and new tools at their disposal.

3

Training and Education

There are various jobs within police departments or investigative agencies that deal with ballistics evidence, and each of them may have a different name and set of responsibilities. In addition, the same job may go by different names depending on which police department or agency you end up working for.

Although this can be confusing, it also means there will be many opportunities out there for those who are willing to be flexible and develop wide-ranging skills. In a situation like this, where there's not one clearly defined career path, your best bet is to assemble a set of skills and training that can be used in a variety of jobs.

Education

According to Dr. Michael Carlie, professor of sociology, anthropology, and criminology at Missouri State University, it is a good idea for anyone interested in forensics to get a solid grounding in science first. A degree in chemistry, biology, or biomedical sciences, combined with a minor in

Forensic pathologist and medical examiner Dr. Werner Spitz points out the possible trajectory of a bullet that killed a murder victim in Michigan in 1999. He based his calculations on the entry and exit points of the bullet.

crime and society or a similar area, is a good foundation for a forensic investigator. After all, a forensic scientist is still a scientist first and foremost and therefore needs to know how to use the tools of observation and experimentation that every scientist employs.

In addition, a forensic ballistics investigator has to understand at least some part of the mathematics of ballistics itself. Trajectory, angle of impact, and other critical data often have to be calculated from the available crime scene evidence. This is the kind of

The American Academy of Forensic Scientists (AAFS)

Since 1948, the AAFS has been an important venue in which forensic scientists from many fields—medicine, dentistry, law, toxicology, anthropology, psychiatry, physics, engineering, education, and more—can find opportunities for professional development, personal contacts, awards, and recognition. Members represent all fifty states, Canada, and fifty-two other countries.

The AAFS is a professional society dedicated to the application of science to the law and criminal justice, the promotion of education, and the insistence upon accuracy, precision, and specificity in the forensic sciences. It publishes the *Journal of Forensic Sciences* and several newsletters, holds an annual scientific meeting, and conducts other seminars and meetings throughout the year. AAFS members receive assistance in finding positions and getting access to important research in their fields.

The AAFS's annual scientific meeting is held every February, during which more than five hundred scientific papers, breakfast seminars, workshops, and other special events are presented. The AAFS is headquartered in Colorado Springs, Colorado.

knowledge that requires a solid background in geometry, trigonometry, and physics.

The American Academy of Forensic Scientists' Web page, www.aafs.org, is an excellent place to learn how to gain solid training for a career in any part of the criminal forensics field. Aside from a bachelor of science degree, with some sort of minor in criminal justice, the academy also recommends that you sharpen your skills as a writer and public speaker, since drafting reports for police and the courts and presenting evidence during trials is likely to be a crucial and substantial part of your job.

According to the AAFS Web site, becoming a forensics investigator requires at least twenty-four semester hours of chemistry or biology, as well as math. Which science degree you obtain is not as important as which courses you take. AAFS also emphasizes that in order to keep up with the many and constant advances in science, you will need to take continuing education courses throughout your entire career.

The AAFS Web site also has links and contact information for many colleges and universities that offer forensic programs, both graduate and undergraduate, inside and outside the United States. Which one you choose should be based on research. Contact the various departments and ask them about their programs; what kind of assistance they offer in getting certifications, internships, and training; and what kind of work their graduates generally go on to do. Along with more day-to-day considerations like geography and finances, this can help you narrow down your choices.

Undergraduate and Graduate Studies

According to Dale Nute, a professor in the School of Criminology and Criminal Justice at Florida State University, it is best to focus on science for your undergraduate degree and get your forensics training as part of a graduate program. He believes this offers the student the best chance to get the necessary grounding in science, gain a good job following graduation, insulate him- or herself from fluctuations in the job market, and position him- or herself for an eventual career in forensics.

In Nute's opinion, the science degree that provides the best foundation in forensics is chemistry. For a ballistics emphasis, good electives could also include optical mineralogy and metallurgy. Whatever courses and electives you take should give you a good basis for examining firearms, bullets, propellants, and chemical reactions during the firing of a gun.

Of course, you will also need a good grounding in basic physics to understand principles of trajectory, flight, arc, ricochet, and other calculations that are included in forensic ballistics. Some academic departments and criminal investigation organizations split "firearms examination" and "forensic ballistics" into separate groups, but some do not, so your best bet is to create a skills set that fulfills the requirements of both categorizations. Flexibility and a broad range of skills make you more employable and offer you a range of job options.

ABC Certifications

Once you have your bachelor's degree, you can become certified by the American Board of Criminalistics (ABC; www.criminalistics.com), which can increase your career opportunities. The ABC offers four levels of certification: diplomate, fellow, technical specialist, and an associate level of pre-certification.

- **Diplomate:** Certification as a diplomate of the ABC (or D-ABC) is awarded to individuals who have a B.S. or B.A. in a natural science, have two years of forensic laboratory experience, and have successfully completed a General Knowledge Examination.

A thorough grounding in a scientific field, such as chemistry, physics, or mathematics, is necessary in order to become a forensic ballistics investigator.

- **Fellow:** Certification as a fellow (F-ABC) is awarded to those who complete the General Knowledge Examination and a relevant examination in their specialty. They must also pass a proficiency test and have a minimum of two years' experience in their specialty area. The specialty areas currently offered are forensic biology, drug analysis, fire debris analysis, and trace evidence.

- **Technical specialist:** Certification as a technical specialist (S-ABC) is awarded to those who complete a written examination. They must also have a B.S. or B.A. in a natural science, have two years' forensic laboratory experience, and have completed a proficiency test within the last twelve months. Technical specialist certifications are currently offered in the specialties of forensic drug analysis and forensic molecular biology.

- **Affiliate:** Individuals who meet all requirements for certification except for the two years of forensic laboratory experience may sit for the General Knowledge Examination. If they pass the examination, they become "Certification Eligible" until they complete their two years' lab experience.

On-the-Job Training

In a field like forensic ballistics, you will obtain most of your basic knowledge while getting your degree or taking continuing education courses—not on the job. Bullet and firearm identification, trajectory calculation, and other techniques require a great deal of training to master. Of course, dealing with real cases will sharpen your skills and expertise and give you the chance to learn from your fellow investigators, who may know techniques and tricks that your

Ballistics investigators often use simple tools, such as string or flags, to help them determine the trajectory of a bullet from evidence left at a crime scene. This investigator is attempting to determine the trajectory of a bullet that left a hole near a murder scene in Columbus, Ohio, in 2003.

instructors did not. If you decide to work in law enforcement before specializing in ballistics, you may get some job training in collecting evidence and interpreting the results of lab tests, depending on your specific job and duties. However, you will still need intensive classroom and lab instruction to qualify as a forensic ballistics investigator.

Building a Career in Forensic Ballistics

Not all forensics investigators started out with the intention of forging a career in this particular branch of the sciences or of criminal justice. Some come into the field from outside disciplines. It is also not unusual for someone to go into forensics as a way of moving up the law enforcement ladder or of changing his or her career focus after many years spent in a police department. Some officers are able to take advantage of CSI courses offered by their state or even the FBI to learn forensic skills. Or they may go back to school to get more advanced science training or an additional degree. They then have the benefit of their earlier experience as police officers to draw on, as well as their new academic training, when applying themselves to a criminal forensics investigation.

Where to Work and for Whom

Which career path you take largely depends on what you want your workplace to be. Forensic ballistics work mostly takes place in a laboratory, and so the most direct route to becoming a forensic ballistics investigator is to start working as a lab scientist directly out of college. Police work takes place in the field. Aside from collecting bullets and seeking out other crime scene evidence, most police officers will not be involved in tasks like comparing bullet striations and calculating trajectories. That is usually left for a specialized forensics team.

In the past, police work and forensic work overlapped more, but that is changing. Like all forensic sciences, ballistics is becoming a more and more advanced specialty. Because new advances and techniques are being discovered all the time, it is a field that requires a great deal of commitment. According to the AAFS, places of employment for forensic ballistics investigators can include the following:

Jason Stenzel, a forensic scientist in Cheney, Washington, uses an infrared spectrometer to do a controlled substance analysis. Spectrometers can also be useful for determining what substances a bullet may have passed through after firing.

- Police departments
- Sheriffs' offices

An Oregon State Police forensic scientist conducts a DNA amplification test in a Portland crime lab. DNA amplification, or "genetic fingerprinting," can be used to match suspects to samples of blood, hair, saliva or semen.

- District attorneys' offices
- Regional and state agencies
- Medical examiners' offices
- Private companies
- Colleges and universities
- Federal agencies such as the Drug Enforcement Administration (DEA), Bureau of Alcohol, Tobacco, Firearms, and Explosives (ATF), Federal Bureau of Identification (FBI), U.S. Postal Service (USPS), Secret Service (SS), Central Intelligence Agency (CIA)

- Branches of the U.S. military (Army, Navy, Air Force, and Marines)
- U.S. Fish and Wildlife Services
- U.S. Department of Justice

After graduating from college, you may start your career as a "bench scientist" in a forensics lab. If you wish, you can set your sights on becoming a lab director, serving local, state, or federal clients. You also may decide to go into academics and teach forensics at a community college or university. What levels you attain will depend on your skills, job satisfaction, and ambition.

The Job Search

As a career, forensic ballistics offers some job security because, unfortunately, gun-related crime is likely to remain common and widespread in North America. Your expertise will be needed almost everywhere. You do not have to limit yourself to one or two areas of the country—or even just North America—to find labs and police departments that need ballistics investigators.

The chemistry department of Eastern Washington University, which offers a degree in forensic chemistry, provides these forensic job search tips:

- Start your job search early, at least six months before you graduate, preferably a year before.

- Jobs do not come to you. Take the initiative and make your own breaks. No one else is going to do it for you.
- Be flexible and seek jobs in different geographical areas. Most forensic lab facilities are found in cities, and you will want (or may be required) to live close to your workplace.
- Work closely with your academic advisor on applications, resumes, and cover letters.
- For a forensic position, you will be required to pass a background check. In many cases, you will have to take a polygraph test. If that presents a problem for you due to a criminal record or a history of drug use, do not apply. Fair or not, this is the way it is, and lying on a job application is against the law.
- Use e-mail, phone, and written letters to communicate with lab directors and other contacts listed in the applications. Be polite and professional, but do not be afraid to ask questions.
- Have realistic expectations of salary. Comparison shop and take into account the cost of living. A starting salary of $40,000 would be great for Spokane, Washington, but not enough to live in a place like San Francisco. Since most forensic jobs are state or federal, there isn't a lot of negotiating room on pay scales. This is not the profession to go into if you wish to get rich.

Lie-detector tests can be an important tool in a criminal investigation, although their results are not always conclusive. A solid criminal case will also include harder evidence, such as ballistics evidence, from the crime scene that can implicate the suspect.

Finally, be adventurous, be patient, be flexible, and trust your instincts. Your first job should be challenging and fun. With a savvy approach and positive attitude, you can find the right job.

5 | The Future of Forensic Ballistics

Ballistics is an evolving field because firearms and bullet types are continuously updated or imported from other countries. However, since the basic equation of "bullet plus gun equals violent crime" is not likely to change in the near future, much of the advances in ballistics are coming from better tracking and identification technologies.

Building Better Databases

We have mentioned national databases such as IBIS and DRUGFIRE that make it easier for federal and state law enforcement agencies to track and identify individual guns and ammunition patterns. But, as computer technology advances, local police departments are starting to become more involved in this work as well.

For example, Forensic Technology, Inc., a private company based in Canada that maintains a ballistics identification database and forensic labs, has recently begun a pilot program with Virginia police departments. Instead of just submitting ballistics information on guns

A forensic ballistics investigator fires an AK-47 automatic assault rifle to determine the signatures of its bullets and shell casings. Ownership and use of AK-47s in the United States is tightly regulated.

obtained from crime scenes, the departments are recording and submitting ballistics information for all guns obtained by their officers—guns discarded in vacant lots or trashcans, found under car seats, or anywhere else.

When a weapon is submitted to Forensic Technology labs, technicians fire it, collect the cartridge casings, and photograph them. The images are then entered into the National Integrated Ballistic Information Network (NIBIN) database, and computers compare them with other images for tiny, unique features. When computers find possible matches, technicians examine the casings to make definitive ones. This database is maintained by Forensic Technology for the U.S. Bureau of Alcohol, Tobacco, Firearms, and Explosives. The program has proven very successful at enabling police to link weapons and crimes that they had not known were related.

Some states have taken other initiatives to track individual guns. Maryland law requires that each new gun sold has one of its fired cartridges photographed and entered into a state database as a form of "ballistic fingerprinting." However, police departments in Maryland do not think this is an entirely effective strategy, saying the database does not produce enough good matches.

Despite the technologically advanced tools at their disposal, forensic ballistics investigators face many challenges. For example, it is easy for a criminal to alter the gun's firing patterns by buying a new replacement barrel, making database information worthless. In those situations, ballistics experts have to rely on other evidence from the crime scene, if any exists.

Sometimes, rather than using chemical tests or microscopes, crucial gun identifications can be made through simply analyzing computer data. For example, law enforcement might keep an eye on a spike in new gun sales (which have to be recorded) and tracking where in a given area discarded guns tend to be recovered. The regional ATF office in Chicago studied the records of hundreds of guns seized from gang members and found that nearly 300 of them had been purchased from just four gun shops in Mississippi.

Above is a collection of guns seized by the Dover, New Hampshire, police in 2004. Many police departments now follow a policy of firing and recording the bullet signatures of any gun seized by the police and entering it into a database to see if it's been linked to any other crimes.

This led to nineteen arrests of people charged with buying and selling massive numbers of guns illegally.

Data Is Not Everything

Despite all the new tools available to local, state, and federal investigators for gathering data on firearms, there is still an urgent need for the required manpower to locate and analyze this data. In 2006, Chicago's ATF received 13,000 gun trace requests from Chicago police. Even if a gun is matched in a database, a forensic ballistics investigator still needs to physically examine and positively identify the gun, if possible. It is far from the easy or instantaneous process that is often depicted on television.

Modified Guns

Depending on the type of gun and the gun parts in question, it is legal for many gun hobbyists to modify their guns' shape or firing function from the standard factory model. However, if one of these legally modified guns is used in a crime, this process can make identification of the gun far more difficult.

Creating, modifying, or repairing firearms is referred to as gunsmithing. A professional gunsmith is required to have a federal license and to record his or her transactions. However, some gun hobbyists do their own gunsmithing for artistic reasons or to affect the range and power of their weapons.

One common modification is "sawing off" a shotgun. Hunting rifles and other shotguns are generally easier to get a license for than handguns. Legally, you need a permit from the Bureau of Alcohol, Tobacco, Firearms, and Explosives to modify your shotgun in this way, but it is not uncommon for illegally modified guns to be used in crimes.

The CSI Effect

Popular shows like *CSI* and *Law & Order* tend to emphasize the glamorous high-tech nature of forensics investigations, while leaving out a lot of the mundane and tedious grunt work. On TV, test results that normally take weeks or months appear in seconds; crime labs are beautifully designed, pristine, and state-of-the-art; and lab scientists get involved in questioning suspects. None of this reflects the real world of crime labs, which are often gritty, underfunded, overwhelmed, at least partially anti-quated, and never in direct contact with crime suspects.

Television forensics programs make investigators seem all-powerful and all-knowing, to the point that some departments now refer to the "CSI effect" when victims and juries expect crime labs to solve cases based on the smallest amount of evidence, just like they do on television. Shows like *CSI* may even be affecting how criminals try to cover their tracks. Some investigators have noticed a rise in the number of cases in which criminals attempt to clean up or destroy all possible DNA evidence clinging to clothes, fabrics, or other surfaces by using bleaches, acids, or other chemi-cally corrosive means.

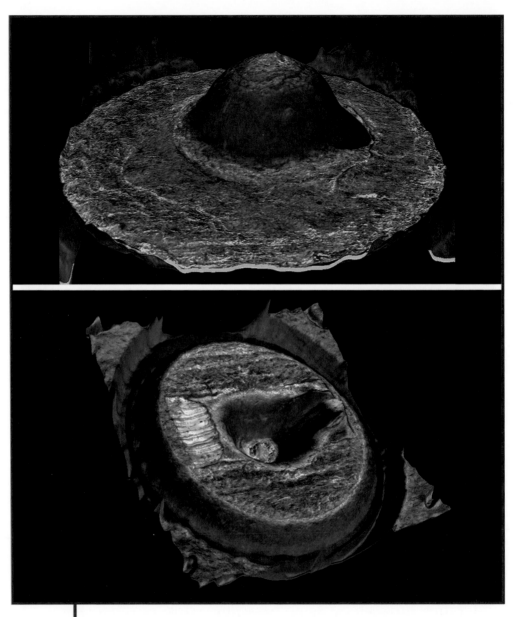

On top is a 3-D image capture of an inverted firing pin impression; at bottom, a 3-D image capture of cartridge case primer. Both of these images can be used to positively identify the cartridge cases from a particular gun, making them invaluable tools in forensic ballistics.

Advances in Weapons

Unlike other areas of forensics, such as DNA identification, the science and technology of ballistics has not changed rapidly in the last few decades. Most of the challenges to a forensic ballistics investigator come in keeping up with new types of bullets, guns, and gun modifications. Since a few popular gun types tend to dominate the market, change has been slow even in this area. An investigator who works on international cases will have to recognize many more gun types than someone who works only on domestic cases. However, as trade and travel increases, so will crime and, more than likely, crime involving weapons manufactured outside the United States.

3-D Bullet Imaging

According to *Wired* magazine, Intelligent Automation, an engineering firm in Montreal, Canada, has developed a way of examining an image of a fired bullet in three dimensions, or 3-D. Called BulletTrax-3D, the new imaging system projects white light through a special microscope onto the bullet or its casing. A camera records the light that is reflected. Then a sophisticated computer program is used to generate a complete 3-D image of the bullet.

One benefit of this technique is that it helps examiners avoid problems they sometimes have with 2-D images. For example, if the image is oriented incorrectly, the examiner might end up comparing different sides, instead of the same sides, of two bullets. With a 3-D image, the researcher will have no trouble keeping the images properly aligned and oriented.

The new images also make it easier to reproduce, store, and send images of a single bullet, increasing the amount of information sharing that can occur between crime labs. The system is already in use at Scotland Yard as well as in Algeria, Australia, India, and other countries. Adoption of this new technology in the United States has been slow because of the high cost and because there are so many 2-D bullet identification programs already in use, many of them sold by Forensic Technologies.

While the 3-D imaging may make matching some bullets easier, according to *Wired*, the research shows that cheaply made bullets from low-quality guns are still hard to identify. It may take yet another leap forward in technology to clear that particular forensics hurdle.

Advances in Computing Power

The expanding power and speed of computers, as well as new technologies that can "sniff out" trace chemicals on spent bullets and wounds, do pose a challenge to an investigator whose training did not include such technology. Learning how to use lab equipment such as gas chromatographs may or may not be part of ballistics investigators' duties, depending on where they work and on their own willingness to learn new skills.

Becoming a forensic ballistics investigator is challenging but rewarding. It is a sad fact of life that guns are likely to be used in crimes for a long time to come, no matter how strictly they are regulated. Guns are too powerful, effective, and readily available for many criminals to resist. However, the advantage that guns lend to criminals can be undermined with a ballistic investigator's knowledge, skill, and determination to put violent offenders behind bars. As a forensic ballistics investigator, you can be someone who makes a difference in the community and the wider world, while helping to protect the safety and peace of your fellow citizens.

automatic/semiautomatic firearms Guns that fire continuously until all ammunition has been used (automatic) or a trigger is released (semiautomatic).

barrel Cylindrical, metal part of a firearm through which the bullet travels.

bench scientist Scientist working in a lab, often with a team of other scientists.

caliber Diameter of the bore (barrel) of a firearm.

criminalistics Also called forensics, the use of scientific techniques to answer questions about biological evidence, trace evidence, impression evidence (such as fingerprints, footwear impressions, and tire tracks), controlled substances, ballistics (firearm examination), and other evidence in criminal investigations.

DNA identification Using the distinctive patterns in a suspect's genetic material to identify whether bodily substances gathered as evidence at a crime scene belong to him or her.

gas chromatograph Machine used to analyze the content of a chemical product or measure toxic substances in soil, air, or water.

gunpowder Explosive mixture that burns rapidly, producing volumes of hot gas that can be used as a propellant in firearms and fireworks. Originally, most gunpowder was made of a nitrate like saltpeter, charcoal, or sulfur. Modern gunpowder uses different chemicals that cause less smoke and corrosion.

primer Explosive that will spark on contact, as when hit with the hammer of a gun trigger. In a gun, that spark will then light the gunpowder that propels the bullet.

rifling Grooves cut inside a rifle barrel that make the bullet spin and travel faster and more accurately.

smooth-bore Older style of shotgun that does not have rifling inside the barrel.

striations Fine lines in the rifling of a firearm caused by the cutting tool. These distinctive markings can help identify the gun and any bullets fired from it but are subject to change over time as more bullets are fired from the gun.

toxicology Study of the adverse effects of chemicals on living organisms. In forensics, this means detecting drugs, poisons, or other substances that were in the victim's body at the time of death.

trajectory Path of a projectile through space.

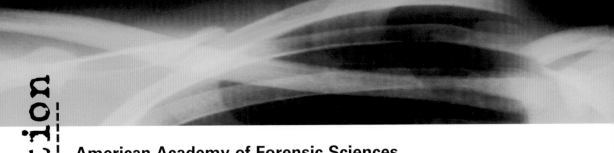

American Academy of Forensic Sciences

410 North 21st Street

Colorado Springs, CO 80904

(719) 636-1100

Web site: http://www.aafs.org

A nonprofit professional society established in 1948 that is devoted to the improvement, the administration, and the achievement of justice through the application of science to the processes of law.

American Society of Crime Laboratory Directors, Inc.

139K Technology Drive

Garner, NC 27529

(919) 773-2044

Web site: http://www.ascld.org

ASCLD is a nonprofit professional society of crime laboratory directors and forensic science managers dedicated to promoting excellence in forensic science through leadership and innovation.

Bureau of Alcohol, Tobacco, Firearms, and Explosives
Firearms Programs Division

650 Massachusetts Avenue NW, Room 7400

Washington, DC 20226

(202) 927-7770

Web site: http://www.atf.treas.gov

ATF is a principal law enforcement agency within the United States Department of Justice dedicated to preventing terrorism, reducing violent crime, and protecting the nation. It is committed to working directly, and through partnerships, to investigate and reduce crime involving firearms and explosives, acts of arson, and illegal trafficking of alcohol and tobacco products.

California Criminalistics Institute

4949 Broadway, Room A104

Sacramento, CA 95820

Web site: http://www.cci.ca.gov

The California Criminalistics Institute, a unit of the California Department of Justice, Bureau of Forensic Services, provides specialized forensic science training to personnel who are practitioners in the field.

Canadian Society of Forensic Science

P.O. Box 37040

3332 McCarthy Road

Ottawa, ON K1V 0W0

Canada

Web site: http://ww2.csfs.ca

A nonprofit professional organization incorporated to maintain professional standards and to promote the study and enhance the stature of forensic science.

Federal Bureau of Investigation

J. Edgar Hoover Building

935 Pennsylvania Avenue NW

Washington, DC 20535-0001

(202) 324-3000

Web site: http://www.fbi.gov

The FBI's mission is to protect and defend the United States against terrorist and foreign intelligence threats, to uphold and enforce the criminal laws of the United States, and to provide leadership and criminal justice services to federal, state, municipal, and international agencies and partners.

International Association for Identification

2535 Pilot Knob Road, Suite 117

Mendota Heights, MN 55120-1120

(651) 681-8566

Web site: http://www.theiai.org

The IAI is committed to associate persons in the forensic science profession, keep them up to date and informed, advance the relevant sciences, encourage research, provide training and education, and the dissemination of this information through its publications thereby fostering a relationship among forensic practitioners worldwide.

Web Sites

Due to the changing nature of Internet links, Rosen Publishing has developed an online list of Web sites related to the subject of this book. The site is updated regularly. Please use this link to access the list:

http://www.rosenlinks.com/cif/bain

For Further Reading

Camenson, Blythe. *Opportunities in Forensic Science Careers.* Chicago, IL: McGraw-Hill, 2001.

Fridell, Ron. *Forensic Science* (Cool Science). Minneapolis, MN: Lerner Publications, 2007.

Platt, Richard. *Crime Scene: The Ultimate Guide to Forensic Science.* New York, NY: Reed Business Information, 2003.

Ragle, Larry. *Crime Scene.* New York, NY: HarperCollins Publishers, 1995.

Ramsland, Katherine M. *Forensic Science of CSI.* New York, NY: Penguin Putnam, Inc., 2001.

Bibliography

Allison, John. "From the Desk of Dr. John Allison." *CSI: Ewing Newsletter: The TCNJ Forensic Chemistry Program.* March 2006. Retrieved August 2007 (http://www.tcnj.edu/ ~csiewing/documents/csiewing4march06.pdf).

CNN.com. "The Real CSI: Investigators' Jobs Less Glamorous, More Personal." May 16, 2005. Retrieved August 6, 2007 (http://www.cnn.com/2005/LAW/05/05/murder.overview/).

CNN.com. "Virginia Tech Shootings Timeline." April 17, 2007. Retrieved August 6, 2007 (http://www.cnn.com/2007/ US/04/17/timeline.text).

Eastern Washington University Forensics Department. "Forensic Jobs and Internships." Retrieved August 6, 2007 (http://www.ewu.edu/x42713.xml).

Evans, Colin. *The Casebook of Forensic Detection: How Science Solved 100 of the World's Most Baffling Crimes.* New York, NY: John Wiley & Sons, Inc., 1996.

Hauser, Christine, and Anahad O'Connor. "Virginia Tech Shooting Leaves 33 Dead." *New York Times.* April 16, 2007. Retrieved August 2007 (http://www.nytimes.com/2007/04/16/us/ 16cnd-shooting.html?ex=1192334400&en=305721272cfa 098d&ei=5087&excamp=GGGNvatechnews).

HowStuffWorks.com. "Firearm Calibers." Retrieved August 6, 2007 (http://www.howstuffworks.com/framed.htm?

parent=question260.htm&url=http://www.gunsandcrime. org/caliber.html).

Linville, Jason, and Ray Liu. "Forensic Science: Fact and Fiction." Science Careers. June 2002. Retrieved August 6, 2007 (http://sciencecareers.sciencemag.org/career_development/ previous_issues/articles/1750/forensic_science_fact_and_ fiction).

Lyle, D. P. *Forensics for Dummies*. Hoboken, NJ: Wiley Publishing, Inc., 1996.

Nickell, Joe, and John F. Fischer. *Crime Science: Methods of Forensic Detection*. Lexington, KY: The University Press of Kentucky, 1999.

O'Connor, T. "MegaLinks in Criminal Justice." Retrieved August 6, 2007 (http://www.apsu.edu/oconnort/default.htm).

Owen, David. *Police Lab: How Forensic Science Tracks Down and Convicts Criminals*. Buffalo, NY: Firefly Books, Inc., 2002.

Roy, Matthew. "Ballistics Database a New Weapon in Solving Crime." *The Virginian-Pilot*. February 27, 2007. Retrieved August 6, 2007 (http://www.forensictechnologyinc.com/c3-n1.html).

Time.com. "Sam Told Me to Do It . . . Sam Is the Devil." August 22, 1977. Retrieved August 6, 2007 (http://www.time.com/time/ magazine/article/0,9171,915296-6,00.html).

G

gauge, defined, 22
General Rifling Characteristics File, 23, 28
Geradts, Zeno, 7–8
Goddard, Calvin Hooker, 11
Gravelle, Philip O., 11
Griess test, 27
guns/gunpowder, history of, 9–10
gunshot residue, analyzing, 25, 26–27, 29
gunshot wounds, analyzing, 25–26, 29
gunsmithing, 48

I

IBIS (Integrated Ballistics Identification System), 28, 44
Intelligent Automation, 51

K

Kennedy, John F., assassination of, 16

M

modified guns, 48, 51
Moskowitz, Stacy, 13

N

National Integrated Ballistic Information Network, 45–46
Nute, Dale, 34

O

on-the-job training, 36–37
Oswald, Lee Harvey, 16

R

rifling of guns, 22–23

S

serial numbers, detecting on gun, 27–28, 29
shell casings, information they reveal, 24
smooth bore firearms, 23–24
Son of Sam case, 13–14

T

3-D bullet imaging, 51–52

V

Virginia Tech, shootings at, 4–6

About the Authors

Between them, Matthew and Janell Broyles have published seven books for Rosen. This is their first collaboration. Janell has published *Chemical and Biological Weapons in a Post 9/11 World*, and Matthew has published *Extreme Careers: Air Marshals*.

Photo Credits